discovermore

Earth's Biomes

A Look at the Taiga

Dwayne Hicks

Britannica
Educational Publishing
IN ASSOCIATION WITH
THE ROSEN PUBLISHING GROUP

Published in 2027 by Britannica Educational Publishing (a trademark of Encyclopædia Britannica, Inc.) in association with The Rosen Publishing Group, Inc.
2544 Clinton Street, Buffalo, NY 14224

Distributed exclusively by Rosen Publishing.
To see additional Britannica Educational Publishing titles, go to rosenpublishing.com.

Editor: Greg Roza
Book Design: Michael Flynn

Photo Credits: Cover GabrijelaZ/Shutterstock.com; (series background) Dai Yim/Shutterstock.com; p. 4 Designua/Shutterstock.com; p. 5 ArtEvent ET/Shutterstock.com; p. 6 adamikarl/Shutterstock.com; p. 7 Victoria Ditkovsky/Shutterstock.com; p. 8 Serg Zastavkin/Shutterstock.com; p. 9 YURY TARANIK/Shutterstock.com; p. 10 Evgeny Ashpin/Shutterstock.com; p. 11 Rennny/Shutterstock.com; p. 12 Pi-Lens/Shutterstock.com; p. 13 DMITRII STARTCEV/Shutterstock.com; p. 15 (top) adamikarl/Shutterstock.com; p. 15 (bottom) Grigorii Pisotsckii/Shutterstock.com; p. 16 Ovchinnikova Irina/Shutterstock.com; p. 17 Barera Studio/Shutterstock.com; p. 18 Kersti Lindstrom/Shutterstock.com; p. 19 SARIN KUNTHONG/Shutterstock.com; p. 20 Piotr Krzeslak/Shutterstock.com; p. 21 (left) Valentin Gazzola/Shutterstock.com; p. 21 (right) ANDREI RASPUTIN/Shutterstock.com; p. 22 Grindstone Media Group/Shutterstock.com; p. 23 Vaclav Sebek/Shutterstock.com; p. 24 Branislav Cerven/Shutterstock.com; p. 25 Maximillian cabinet/Shutterstock.com; p. 26 Spiridon Sleptsov/Shutterstock.com; p. 27 SL-Photography/Shutterstock.com; p. 28 Kim Kuperkova/Shutterstock.com; p. 29 soul_studio/Shutterstock.com.

Cataloging-in-Publication Data

Names: Hicks, Dwayne.
Title: A look at taiga / Dwayne Hicks.
Description: New York : Britannica Educational Publishing, in association with Rosen Educational Services, 2027. | Series: Discover more: Earth's biomes | Includes glossary and index.
Identifiers: ISBN 9781641906357 (library bound) | ISBN 9781641906340 (pbk) | ISBN 9781641906364 (ebook)
Subjects: LCSH: Taiga ecology--Juvenile literature. | Biotic communities--Juvenile literature.
Classification: LCC QH541.5.T3 H68 2027 | DDC 577.37--dc23

Manufactured in the United States of America

Some of the images in this book illustrate individuals who are models. The depictions do not imply actual situations or events.

CPSIA Compliance Information: Batch #CSBRIT27. For further information contact Rosen Publishing at 1-800-237-9932.

Contents

Forests of the North

Earth is a planet of diversity. Plants and animals of all different shapes, colors, and sizes are spread all over the planet in Earth's biomes! A biome is a large region, or part, of Earth that has a certain climate and certain types of living things. Major biomes include forests, grasslands, tundra, and deserts.

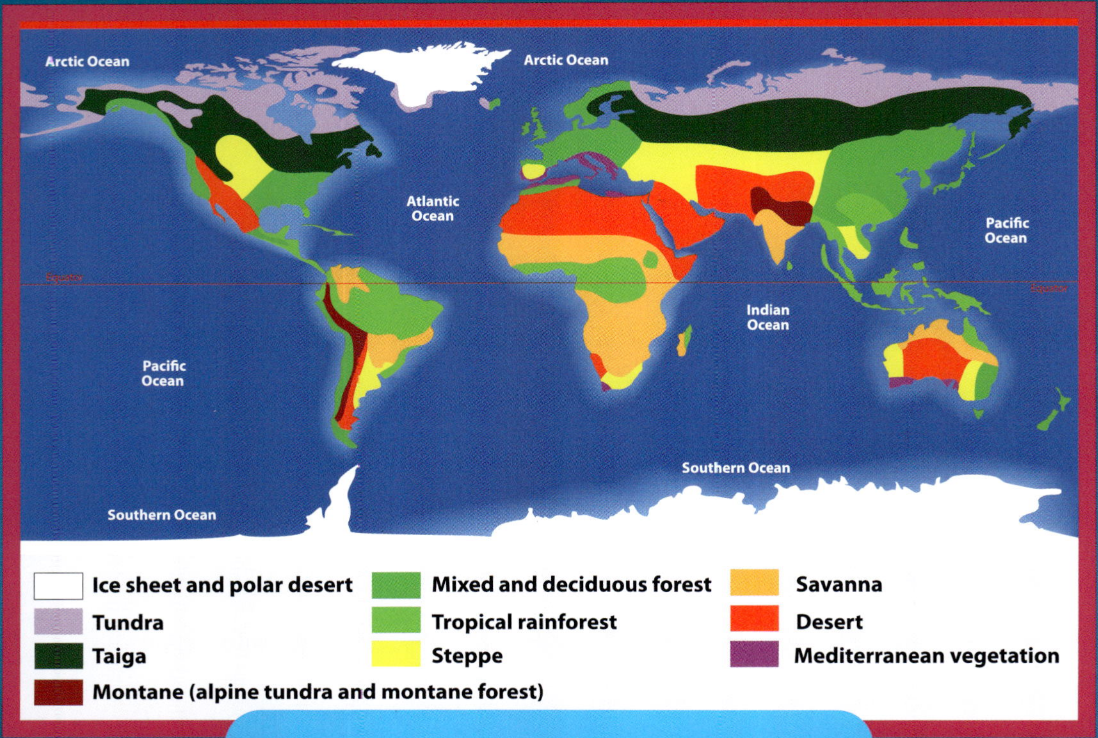

This map shows Earth's major biomes.

The taiga stretches for miles and miles in North America.

One of the world's largest land biomes is the taiga. The taiga is a forest biome. Another name for the taiga is boreal forest. (The word "boreal" is used to describe the northern areas of Earth just south of the Arctic.) The trees in these forests are mostly conifers. Conifers, such as pine trees and fir trees, have needle-shaped leaves. Most conifers keep their leaves year-round.

The taiga is known for its extreme cold. Summers are short and winters are long. This makes life for plants, animals, and people difficult.

Consider This

The taiga is one type of forest. Can you think of other types? What are some differences and similarities?

Where Is the Taiga?

The taiga is located south of the tundra. The tundra is a biome known for being a cold, treeless, barren land. The taiga is located north of the deciduous forests of temperate regions.

In winter, the taiga forests of Riisitunturi National Park in Finland become blanketed in heavy snow.

In summer, the taiga in Alberta, Canada, is a popular destination for camping, hiking, and canoeing.

The taiga spans across northern Europe, Asia, and North America. Russia's taiga stretches about 3,600 miles (5,800 kilometers) across the country! The taiga exists in Canada, Scandinavia, Alaska, and Siberia. Siberia is a northern region in Russia. Siberia is a classic taiga region known for its bitterly cold winters.

There aren't many big cities in the taiga. However, Toronto, Canada, and Moscow, Russia, are major cities that thrive in the taiga. Moscow has a **population** of around 13 million people! The Toronto area is home to about 7 million people.

WORD WISE

POPULATION IS THE NUMBER OF PEOPLE LIVING IN AN AREA.

Trees and Glaciers

The taiga is dominated by vast conifer forests. The forests are thicker in the southern taiga, where temperatures are not so extreme. Other taiga features include canyons and plateaus, as well as mountains and valleys. For example, Canada's taiga contains an area called the Taiga Cordillera. It is part of the Rocky Mountains. In addition to the tall mountains, it has high waterfalls, deep canyons, and rivers.

The East Siberia taiga in Russia covers approximately 5.7 million square miles (14.8 million sq km). It's the largest forest biome in the world.

Glaciers carved out taiga land as they grew, and left behind lakes when they melted.

Some landforms are created by weathering and erosion. Weathering is the breaking down of rocks, while erosion is the carrying away of weathered rock. Taiga rivers help shape the land through erosion. Many taiga landforms were caused by erosion from glaciers, or large, moving sheets of ice. Much of the taiga was completely covered in glaciers during the last **ice age** thousands of years ago. The glaciers shaped the land as they moved.

WORD WISE

AN ICE AGE IS A TIME WHEN GLACIERS COVER HUGE AREAS OF LAND.

A Soggy Biome

Some parts of the taiga receive more than 40 inches (100 centimeters) of precipitation a year. This makes it a wet biome, whereas the tundra to the north is almost a desert in some places.

When glaciers cut through the taiga, they left behind areas that are now lakes, wetlands, and ponds. The taiga has a few large river systems, mostly in Siberia. This region is home to the Lena, Yenisey, and Ob Rivers. These waterways and bodies of water support many plants and animals.

In winter, much of the tiaga is snow-covered.

These muskegs are a common sight in the taiga of southern Alaska.

The taiga has a very thin layer of soil. It often has **permafrost** or bedrock just underneath the soil. That makes it nearly impossible for water to drain through the soil in some places. The water pools up and forms shallow bogs, or wet muddy ground. These spongy, wet areas are called muskegs.

WORD WISE

PERMAFROST IS A LAYER OF PERMANENTLY FROZEN GROUND THAT IS LOCATED BELOW THE SOIL IN FAR NORTHERN REGIONS.

A Cold Biome

Earth's different biomes experience a wide range of weather conditions. Many places experience different temperatures as the seasons change. However, the closer a region is to the poles, the more extreme the changes are.

In some taiga areas, wildflowers bloom in summer, attracting insects and birds to the area.

Winter is a hard time in the taiga. Temperatures below zero are common and snowfall is high.

The taiga has short summers. The temperatures are mild, or not too warm or cold. The average temperature in summer is between 59 and 68 °F (15 and 20 °C). The biome receives a lot of precipitation in the form of rain. Some animals move to the taiga for a time during the summer.

When winter hits the taiga, winds from the Arctic bring very cold weather. Winter weather often lasts about seven months. Due to the Earth tilting away from the sun, winter days in the taiga are short, and the nights are long. Temperatures can drop to -65 °F (-54 °C). This deadly cold keeps many people and animals hidden away, waiting out the winter.

Consider This

What would it be like to live in subzero temperatures most of the year? How would you have to prepare?

Coniferous Trees

Temperate forests are found south of the taiga. They are also called deciduous forests. Deciduous trees lose and regrow leaves throughout the seasons. They often have wide, flat leaves.

The forests of the taiga are different from temperate forests. Taiga forests are coniferous. Conifers are trees that form seeds inside cones. Conifers in the taiga include pines, spruces, larches, and firs. Conifer leaves are small and needle shaped. Larches lose their needle, but other conifers keep theirs when the seasons change.

Conifers have features that help them to survive the cold, snowy climate of the taiga. Conifers are shaped like cones with branches that point downward. This allows snow to slide off easily. The leaves are dark green. This means they have more of the substance that allows green plants to soak in sunlight. This allows them to absorb as much sunlight as they can during the short summer.

Conifers are also called evergreen trees because their leaves don't change color during the year.

compare and contrast

What are the similarities between deciduous and coniferous forests? What are the differences?

A conifer cone holds seeds. It can take up to 3 years for a conifer cone to finish growing before it releases seeds.

Other Taiga Plants

The taiga forests have much less wildlife diversity compared to tropical or temperate forests. One reason for the lack of diversity is the harsh weather. Another reason is the taiga soil. Taiga soil is high in acid. It has very few nutrients. It is also thin, often with rocky layers just underneath. That makes it hard for roots to take hold and for plants to grow.

Low shrubs, such as this flowering rosemary, survive well in the taiga.

Lingonberry bushes are native to the boreal forests. They are particularly popular in Scandinavian dishes.

The smaller plants that exist in the taiga have had to adapt to the climate, just like the conifers there. Many plants are low to the forest floor. Low shrubs grow in some parts of the taiga. Some of the shrubs produce berries, such as lingonberries, blueberries, currants, and cloudberries. Mosses and **lichens** grow on tree trunks, rocks, and the ground.

WORD WISE

LICHENS ARE PLANT-LIKE LIVING THINGS THAT ARE MADE UP OF TWO TINY LIVING THINGS: A FUNGUS AND AN ALGA.

Taiga Animals

The taiga also has low animal diversity. That means the taiga has fewer kinds of animals than most other biomes. Two reasons for this are the harsh climate and the lack of plants to eat.

Caribou, also called reindeer, thrive in the taiga and tundra areas.

The taiga flycatcher spends winter in Southeast Asia. In summer, it flies to the taiga in eastern Siberia to feast on insects.

Taiga mammals include large ungulates, or animals with hooves, such as moose and caribou. They also include predators such as lynx, bears, and wolves. Smaller mammals include martens, northern flying squirrels, beavers, and muskrats.

If you visit the taiga during its warmer months, you'll find more animal diversity. Many bird species, for example, come to the taiga just for the summer. Just like taiga plants, animals in this biome must adapt to the weather and land features of the taiga.

Consider This

Why might you find more animals in the taiga during the warmer months?

While many animals couldn't survive a taiga winter, native animals have the adaptations necessary to keep them alive. Some taiga animals hibernate, or spend the winter in a sleep-like state. Hibernating animals don't move much to save energy. They don't eat either. They find a warm burrow or cave and wait for spring.

The gray wolf's thick fur keeps it warm and dry through the long taiga winter.

The ermine, a type of weasel, has fur that turns snow white in winter. This helps it hide from predators all year long.

Most taiga animals have thick fur. It insulates the animal's body to keep the cold out. Gray wolves have two kinds of fur in their coat: insulating fur and moisture-repellant fur. Moose have one layer of woolly fur that provides extra warmth and a top layer that traps air and helps the moose swim. Many taiga animals' coats also change color in the winter to provide them with **camouflage**.

WORD WISE

CAMOUFLAGE IS THE HIDING OR DISGUISING OF SOMETHING BY COVERING IT UP OR CHANGING THE WAY IT LOOKS.

Taiga Hunters

Food chains describe the order in which organisms, or living things, depend on each other for food. Predators are the animals that eat other animals in a food chain. Like all biomes, the taiga has many food chains.

Taiga predators have adaptations that make them great hunters. Wolves are highly intelligent animals and skilled hunters. Wolves in the taiga are gray or white. Coat colors are lighter in snowier areas for camouflage. Their fur is very thick to keep out the cold.

The color of a lynx's fur allows it to blend into its surroundings as it stalks its prey.

The large paws of the Siberian tiger are a lot like snowshoes. They help the tiger walk in deep snow.

Lynx are wild cats. They have long limbs, tufted ears, and large paws adapted for moving over the snow. Their cream-colored, spotted coats act as camouflage. They have very sharp eyesight for finding prey.

Siberian tigers are also wild cats. In fact, this species of tiger is the world's largest cat. These tigers live mainly in the forests of Russia. Their fur is longer, softer, and paler than that of other kinds of tigers.

Consider This

How do predators in the taiga take advantage of their fur color to hunt?

On the Move

Migration is an adaptation that allows many kinds of animals to survive. Some animals enjoy the taiga during its fair weather summer. They are able to find their way to more suitable conditions during the taiga's bitter winter.

Some kinds of birds live their whole lives in the taiga. The capercaillie or taiga grouse can be found in much of Russia and Scandinavia, as well as parts of Europe.

The most common insect in the taiga is the mosquito. You may also spot flies, moths, wood-boring beetles, and bees during the warm months.

In the spring, billions of birds begin their journey to the taiga. Some birds come to taiga forests to breed. Waterfowl enjoy the many lakes and rivers of the taiga. Many insects breed in muskegs and wetlands, providing food for migrating birds. Seasonal birds include grouse, warblers, sandpipers, woodpeckers, and gulls. In fall, the insects die off and the birds begin their journey to warmer places to ride out the winter.

WORD WISE

MIGRATION IS MOVING FROM ONE PLACE TO ANOTHER AT CERTAIN TIMES OF THE YEAR. ANIMALS MIGRATE TO BREED OR TO FIND FOOD.

The Icy Life

Just like the plants and animals native to the taiga, people who live in the taiga have adapted to its climate and landscape. Some **indigenous peoples** have lived there for thousands of years.

Taiga tribes in Siberia used to be nomadic, which means they moved around a lot looking for food. Today most live in settlements. The Sakha and Komi peoples now have their own republics within Russia. There are hundreds of indigenous communities in Canada's taiga.

The Republic of Sakha is Russia's largest federal district. The Sakha people have lived in this area for hundreds of years.

Indigenous Canadians catch salmon from Bulkley River in British Columbia, Canada.

How do these peoples survive? They make use of what they have. Some herd reindeer and rely on hunting and gathering for food. Some fish in the summer and ice fish in the winter. Some hunt mammals from beaver and rabbit to caribou and moose. Some make use of the trees and shrubs to make tools, shelter, and medicine. Some communities are cut off from the world for the whole winter. They rely on each other to get them through the cold season.

WORD WISE

INDIGENOUS PEOPLES ARE GROUPS WHO ARE NATIVE TO A REGION.

Respecting the Taiga

Even though many plants, animals, and people have adapted to life in the taiga, the biome is in danger, mainly because of the actions of people. Deforestation is one of the greatest dangers to the taiga. It means cutting down large amounts of trees, often for lumber, cardboard, and paper. Sometimes, all the trees in a certain area are taken away. The animals that call these trees home are then homeless. Without trees to stop erosion and flooding, the soil is swept away and only empty land is left.

Logging is big business in Canada! But deforestation is a huge threat to the Canadia taiga.

The taiga is especially at risk because of climate change. As global temperatures rise, the permafrost starts to thaw and turn into bogs. New species move into the taiga. These push out the native plants and animals that are already living there. Animals that are built for cold weather can't adapt to warmer weather. This unique biome could change forever unless people treat the taiga with respect and care.

Consider This

Why do you think forest animals need trees to survive? How does cutting down trees affect these animals?

Glossary

absorb To take in.
adapt To change so as to fit a new or specific use for a situation.
barren Having little or no living things.
breed To come together to produce offspring.
climate The average weather conditions of a particular place or region over a long period.
climate change Changes in Earth's weather patterns, including rising temperatures, believed to be caused by human actions.
coniferous Relating to an order of mostly evergreen trees and shrubs having needle or scale-like leaves.
deciduous Relating to trees or plants with leaves that fall off or shed seasonally.
diversity The condition of having a range or mix of different parts.
extreme Existing to a very great degree.
feature A part or detail of something that stands out.
harsh Disagreeable, or causing discomfort.
insulate To prevent the transfer of heat.
plateau A broad flat area of high land.
pole One of the two ends of Earth's axis. The axis is an imaginary line through the center of Earth, around which the planet rotates. The two ends are the North Pole and the South Pole.
precipitation Water or the amount of water that falls to earth as hail, mist, rain, sleet, or snow.
repellant Serving to drive something away, such as water.
republic A political unit.
temperate Having a climate that is usually not too hot or cold.
waterfowl A bird that is found in or near water.

For More Information

Books

Animal Reads staff. *All Things Reindeer for Kids.* Macomb, MI: Admore Publishing, 2025.

Buckley, A. W. *Biomes.* North Mankato, MN, ABDO Books, 2024.

Websites

Reindeer Facts for Kids
kids.kiddle.co/Reindeer
Read all about reindeer here!

World Biomes and Ecosystems
www.ducksters.com/science/ecosystems/world_biomes.php
The Ducksters website has tons of fascinating information about Earth's biomes and ecosystems.

Index